THE ART
UNLEARN

THE ART OF UNLEARNING

TIM COOPER

StoryTerrace®

Text Nuala Calvi on behalf of Story Terrace

Design Grade Design and Adeline Media, London

Copyright © Tim Cooper & Story Terrace

Text is private and confidential

First print August 2018

Story Terrace·

www.StoryTerrace.com

CONTENTS

'The good thing about the start is that you're never there again.' Tim Cooper

PROLOGUE

successful life is not built on your ability to *add*, but on your ability to *remove*.

After spending years judging my success (and others') on the volume of shiny objects I had, I realised that attaching happiness to material things – or even to a specific outcome, in fact – is a recipe for disaster. Obsessively chasing that next promotion or collecting designer watches might seem like the mark of a winner, but if you need to have something in your life in order for you to be happy – if you are attaching your happiness to external factors – you will always be searching for that next hit of dopamine. It's like an addiction: you're always chasing that first-ever feeling of euphoria, and the satisfaction you derive becomes less and less every time.

It wasn't until I lost what I thought was everything – until my career and my material possessions were stripped away – that I claimed back my true values and gained clarity, perspective and gratitude for all that I had. I was forced into a position that made me see the world through a different set of eyes and appreciate the small pleasures in life. As a result of my own experience, I now see that it's the simplicity and fundamentals of life that hold true beauty. You don't need more, you need less.

I'm not just talking in terms of material possessions. In today's world most of us are searching for a new tool, a new skill, more information, more knowledge – but everything we need is already inside of us. Under all the layers of fear and self-doubt, our true potential is already there, waiting for us to uncover it. It's not until we remove what's not serving us that we can see clearly what truly matters.

As I set out on my own journey, I soon came to realise that the best things in life aren't *things* at all. They are people. They are experiences.

It's time to unlearn everything that is false and unhelpful and make way for the real you to shine.

'Success is not final, failure is not fatal: it is the courage to continue that counts.'
Winston Churchill

1

THE DAY I DECIDED TO DIE

March 10th 2016 is a memorable day for me. It was going to be my last day. It was going to be the day I killed myself.

Of course, killing myself didn't just occur to me out of the blue that morning. I didn't just wake up with a random death wish. That feeling had been slowly growing inside of me over several weeks and months, ever since my wife had left me.

I was married for 18 months, to the woman I believed was the love of my life. I had a picture-perfect life with her: a big house, three sports cars on the drive, a six-figure salary. I thought I had it all, and then I lost it.

I lost the wife. I lost the job. Without the job I couldn't pay for the cars, so one by one those started to go. The divorce was going through, the house was on the market. As the life I had built for myself unravelled, the idea of just ending it all gradually took hold. It grew like a cancer in my brain.

I began to fantasise about the different ways I could do it. I'm scared of heights, so jumping off a tall building wasn't an option. I didn't want to jump in front of a train – I wanted to be in control. I looked at the last remaining car on the drive, my beautiful white Mercedes-AMG C63. It could go from 0 to 60 in four seconds. All I had to do was put my foot down on the accelerator, hard, and drive that baby into a wall. I knew the perfect place, too. Just off a roundabout near my house in Broxbourne, Hertfordshire, where there was a nice big wall by a bus stop.

That day, March 10th, I woke up late. My head was pounding, my nose was bunged up. I was weak and shaky. All around me was the evidence of what I had been doing the night before: rolled up bank notes, credit cards, white powder on the coffee table. My vinyl records were strewn all over the place, empty bottles lay on the floor, the sink was full of dirty glasses. As usual, I had been doing my best to party myself into oblivion.

Hunger kicked in. I couldn't remember the last time I had eaten, and there was no food in the house. I threw on some dirty clothes, hid my bloodshot eyes behind a pair of sunglasses, and got into the car.

I went to a drive-through McDonalds and ordered two McFlurries. As I waited for them, I looked around at my £60,000 Mercedes. It was a filthy mess. There was rubbish everywhere and it hadn't been cleaned in months. Then I looked in the mirror. I was even more of a mess. My hair was greasy and unwashed, my chin was full of stubble. I took the McFlurries with a pang of shame.

As I turned back onto the road my mind was racing. *You're a wreck*, I told myself. *Look at the state of you and what you're eating. Look at the state of this beautiful car. Look at the state your life has become. You're a total failure, Tim Cooper. You've let yourself and everyone else down. Now's the time to put that plan of yours into action.*

I turned back onto the road and started driving towards the roundabout, the one I had been thinking about all those weeks. I opened the car windows and put the roof down. As the air rushed past my face, I filled my lungs and shouted my pain into the wind.

I turned off the roundabout, and as the wall by the bus stop came into view, I undid my seatbelt. Then I slammed my foot down on the accelerator. I felt the car growl in response, the powerful engine roaring into action. It was a 30-mile-an-hour zone but I was doing 50, then 60, then 70 – hurtling towards the wall.

But suddenly, it felt like I was only doing five miles an hour. Life went into slow motion, and as I crept along the road, I visualised what was about to happen. I saw the Mercedes smashing into the wall in front of me. I saw myself flying out of the seat and crumpling against the wall. And then it was my funeral, and all my family – my mum, dad and sister – were standing over my coffin.

"Tim just couldn't take it anymore," they were saying. "Tim had so much potential, but he couldn't get over his marriage ending and losing it all. It just got the better of him."

I saw their faces, I saw the tears in their eyes, and I felt disappointment. Disappointment in myself. I knew I couldn't do this to them. Somehow, I would have to fight this. I would have to claw my way back.

I put my foot down on the brake, and as the car slowed, life sped up again. I drove a few hundred yards down the road, then pulled over and began to sob.

I sobbed for about 20 minutes. A grown man, in a Mercedes, crying like a baby. But I was crying with gratitude, for the fact that coming so close to death had somehow given me the will to carry on living.

Instead of driving into that wall, I drove to my parents' house. And when my mum opened the door, I told her the truth for the first time. I told her how I'd lost everything, and how I'd lost myself along the way. How I'd got to the point where I didn't even value my own life anymore.

My mum's face when I told her that was devastating to see, but not as devastating as it had been when I'd seen her looking at her son's coffin.

"I'm so sorry," I said. "I'm so sorry for who I've become, because it's not who you brought me up to be. I promise you I'm going to find my way back, and I'm going to be a better person."

That day, March 10th – the day I was going to kill myself – turned out to be the first day of the rest of my life. I kept my promise to my mum, although the journey wasn't always easy. And in this book, I'm going to tell you how I did it.

How I went from someone who didn't even think his life was worth living, to someone who wakes up every day full of joy and gratitude for every breath he takes. How someone who thought he had lost everything discovered that he hadn't even found out what really mattered yet.

I'm going to show you how finding out what your true values are, finding your real purpose in life and finding the right coach to help you achieve the life of your dreams can make the difference between really living and just existing. I'm going to show you that, no matter how deep the hole you've got into, no matter how bleak the future seems, you can get out and you can find a life worth living.

Trust me. I've done it.

'Childhood means simplicity. Look at the world with the child's eye - it is very beautiful.'
Kailash Satyarthi

2

HE IMPORTANCE OF KNOWING AND BEING TRUE TO YOUR VALUES

So, how did I get to the point of wanting to slam myself into a wall? What had gone so badly wrong in my life that I thought it wasn't worth living? Was there something deep within me, perhaps something originating in my childhood – was I unloved, neglected, abused?

No. I was a normal person, from a normal family. OK, we weren't rich – in fact, my parents had very little money, but they were hard workers, and they loved my sister and me with all their hearts. What went so wrong was that, along the way, I lost touch with my values – the values that my parents had instilled in me.

Both my parents had it pretty tough growing up. My mum's mum had to bring up five kids on her own, working like crazy to support them all. My dad lost his own mum when he was very young. They grew up knowing the value of hard work, of being grateful for what you had. And above all, they were savers. "Never have any debt hanging over your head," was my mum's motto. "Save, save, save."

They lived by that mantra. My dad was a haulage driver, and my mum a secretary. If we wanted to go on holiday, they set up a holiday fund six months in advance. Their dream was to own their own bungalow, and they saved for years to get it, selling their car for the deposit. Then they saved for all the bits and pieces to go into it – everything from the door handles to the front gate. They did it by cutting back – cutting back on the holidays, even cutting back on food sometimes. But when they finally got there they couldn't have been prouder. It wasn't Buckingham Palace, but my mum kept it as clean as if the Queen was going to visit any day.

Those were the values I'd been brought up with, but fate took me down another path. In my 20s, I was working as a salesman in the hair and beauty industry. One day after work I was having dinner with a friend at Pizza Express when a beautiful young woman walked past the window – and changed my life. She had sleek blonde hair and she was wearing a stylish monochrome dress with knee-high black boots. The fork stopped halfway to my mouth.

"Jesus," I said. "She's amazing."

I saw the girl going into a bar nearby, so my friend and I followed. She was chatting to someone I knew from my gym, and when he went to the bar to get a drink, I cornered him.

"Who's that girl?" I asked.

"Oh, that's Claire," he said. "She owns a couple of

hairdressing salons round here."

I was instantly impressed. The girl looked no older than me, yet she already had two salons of her own.

I wasted no time in going up to her and telling her I worked in the hair industry and that, funnily enough, I had an appointment at her salon the next day. I'm sure she knew it was a lie, but she went along with it, and the next day I arrived for my 'appointment'.

When I walked into the salon, I could see that the whole place revolved around Claire. Everyone was running around asking her questions, wanting her opinion, and she was in command of it all. She was well spoken, with an accent that suggested private school, and everything about her oozed confidence and success – from the way she carried herself to the Rolex on her wrist and the Mercedes convertible parked outside. I was completely bowled over, and I couldn't believe it when *she* asked *me* out on a date.

But dating Claire wasn't like dating any girl I'd met before. First there was the kind of places we went to. Not just any restaurants, but Harvey Nichols, The Ivy, Claridge's, The Ritz. We drank at the International Champagne Bar on St Martin's Lane, or Annabel's in Mayfair. Sometimes Claire paid for me, which made me feel bad.

I wanted to impress her, and I could see that she loved designer clothes. I began eating up my salary buying her dresses from Vivian Westwood and Valentino, and shoes from Jimmy Choo. It was an expensive business. Not that she ever asked me to buy her anything – I put the pressure on myself to match what I imagined were her expectations.

Luckily, I soon had a new, better-paid job to help fund my new lifestyle. Claire's dad, who had a multimillion-pound solar energy business, took me on in his sales team. Determined to prove myself worthy of the opportunity, I worked like mad to pull in sales – and earned myself a very healthy commission.

But at dinners with Claire's family and friends I was still painfully aware of being the boy from the wrong side of the tracks. Suddenly I was in a world of people who had £6 million houses and drove Ferraris. I caused raised eyebrows when I put my elbows on the table, blew my nose at dinner or left my knife and fork on the wrong place on the plate. I wasn't used to each dish being served at the table – my mum had always just handed us a plate of food each – so I got nervous about taking too much and spilt the gravy everywhere.

Certain people in Claire's circle did their best to make me feel as small as possible, rolling their eyes at my dinner table faux pas and expressing astonishment that I hadn't been to an exclusive holiday resort or hadn't heard of an expensive type of wine. Their sneering drove me on, making me determined to prove my worth on their terms – by acquiring the same material things that they all had.

So I worked harder, and brought in ever more commission. Claire's dad's business was booming and I was earning more than my parents ever had in their lives. He had a friend at Hatton Garden who often visited, and the next time I saw him, I decided to reward myself with my very first Rolex. Even on what I was earning, it had to be on credit, but I didn't care. As I strapped that luxury watch with its salmon dial and diamond bezel onto my wrist, I told myself this was it: I was becoming a somebody.

But I soon discovered it wasn't enough to have just one watch – you had to have two or three. I began rotating the Rolex with a Breitling and a Panerai. I started wearing designer clothes like everyone around me, telling myself that if I dressed this way, people would look at me differently. And they did – at least, the people who had bought into the same mindset I now had.

Claire's sister was always getting expensive gifts from her husband on special occasions, so I made sure that on Valentine's Day, Claire got a pair of £2,000 diamond earrings. When I proposed to her, I took out a loan and bought her a £10,000 diamond ring. On our wedding day she got a £6,000 diamond bracelet to go with it. The woman was dripping in diamonds – but it was OK, my salary was covering the repayments. Just.

We bought a huge house together (helped, of course, by Claire's dad) complete with its own gym. Soon we had the sports cars on the drive like everyone else – a Mercedes, an Aston Martin and my favourite, a beautiful white Porsche – all on credit, with jaw-dropping monthly repayments.

We honeymooned in Saint Tropez and holidayed in five-star hotels around the world, always flying business class –

even when we went to South Africa and it cost £10,000 each. For a boy who'd had to go hungry for a door handle it was like being handed the golden ticket to Willy Wonka's chocolate factory. It was a life beyond my wildest dreams, and I was determined to live it to the fullest. Not only that, but I was determined to stick it to all the snobs around me who treated me like I wasn't good enough.

Yet I was on a constant treadmill, desperately trying to keep my commission soaring higher and higher in order to keep up with the Joneses. I was pulling in a six-figure salary at Claire's dad's, but soon even that couldn't cover the monthly repayments for all the shiny new things I had bought. I began to panic. I realised I was going to have to pull something else out of the bag, so I began to do deals on the side to bring in a bit of extra cash. I felt trapped, like an animal in a cage. I wasn't happy, but I realised now there was no way I could ever escape from this life. If I left the job at Claire's dad's then I wouldn't be able to keep up with my monthly repayments. I was stuck.

And then it all came crashing down around me.

Claire left. She left, and she got together with someone else. And then the job with her dad was gone. Suddenly it was just me, alone in a massive house with three sports cars on the drive that I had no way of paying for.

Bit by bit, everything had to go. The watches. The jewellery. The cars. Worst of all, the beautiful white Porsche. I drove it back myself and signed it over. I had driven it out of the showroom brand new, and now the Porsche rep went over the bodywork inch by inch, picking out every little scratch and telling me it would cost even more. As he spoke I felt physically sick.

I got the train back, and that's when I went into a deep hole. Yes, it was only a car, but for me it was so much more. It had been my proof that I'd made it, that I was somebody worth knowing. Now all those people who had looked down their noses at me would be laughing, thinking they had been right all along. I was a failure. I was a nothing.

I walked into the empty house, dropped to the floor and curled up in a ball. *That's it for me*, I thought. *My world has ended. My life is over.*

And I was right, in a way. The life I had bought into was over. The me that I had constructed from the flimsy material of social status and money had disappeared. But there was another me, a me I had to get to know again, once all the trappings of success were stripped away. I had to get back in touch with who he was and what his true values were. The values that my parents had instilled in me all those years ago. The values I had lost sight of in the glare of all the shiny objects I had bought and lost.

The best things in life, I was to discover, are not things at all. And my true life had barely even begun. But I had a very rocky road to travel before I would realise that.

'One of the most beautiful qualities of true friendship is to understand and to be understood.'
Lucius Annaeus Seneca

3

CHANGING YOUR ENVIRONMENT AND SURROUNDING YOURSELF WITH THE RIGHT PEOPLE

It's when your life comes crashing down around you that you really find out who your friends are.

The day my wife left me, I went to see one of my best friends. I told him what had happened, and his response was, "Well, I knew it wouldn't last." He didn't just mean the relationship. He meant the whole lifestyle I'd been leading. A lifestyle all my friends had been jealous of for a long time.

Now I was losing all the things they'd been jealous of, and it made them feel better. It put me back in my place, and they could all have a good laugh at my expense. Not one of them was there for me. Not one of them picked up the phone to check if I was OK.

I left my friend's house feeling even worse than I had before. On the way home, I went to see a local dealer and bought some cocaine.

When I got in I put a record on, really loud. I snorted some coke, and then I began ransacking all the expensive booze that Claire and I had acquired over the years. There was a lot of it. Wine, Champagne, spirits. Whatever – I didn't care. All I wanted to do was to blot out the pain I was feeling.

As I drank, I cried. I turned the music up louder, and I cried louder. I was desperate for something – anything – to take this suffering away. This hollow, aching feeling of loneliness, despair and self-loathing.

I went online, not knowing what I was searching for. I just knew I couldn't be on my own a minute longer. I needed company. So I did something I'd never done before, something I'd never even have considered: I called a prostitute.

The girl came round, and for about four hours I talked and cried on her, and we drank and sniffed coke together. I told her all about Claire, all about how I was getting divorced. Before she left we had sex, and after she was gone I carried on drinking and snorting coke on my own.

The next few days passed in a haze. More booze, more drugs, more prostitutes. I was on a serious self-destruction mission, so full of despair that I didn't care if I overdosed or got alcohol poisoning. I almost willed it to happen.

That set the tone for the weeks and months to come, as I lurched from one hangover and comedown to another. I managed to get a job selling cars through a former work contact, but I soon lost it after I frequently turned up late or called in sick thanks to my alcohol and drug abuse.

When the house sale went through, I found myself with a

little bit of money in my pocket after all my loans had been paid off. To me, it was just more fuel for the fire of my self-destruction. The friends who'd offered me no emotional support before were now more than happy to go along for the ride, especially if I was paying. They'd come knocking for me, inviting me to the local pub for the first few drinks of the night. Then I'd buy more alcohol to take back to mine and score some coke on the way. We'd stay up all night getting off our faces and calling my dealer whenever we ran out. Soon I was spending hundreds and hundreds of pounds on coke every week.

In the early hours, when my friends left, I'd stave off the loneliness by calling prostitutes again. Some of the girls also sold drugs, so I'd buy more from them, and the whole thing would start up all over again. The next time I saw my friends they would remark on what a great night it had been, but for me the party never ended between one bender and the next.

It was after a particularly bad night of excess that I had woken up and decided to kill myself. After I turned up at my mum's house that day and admitted what a mess I was in, I Googled, in my desperation, *How to fix yourself when you're at rock bottom*. One of the links that came up was to a video on YouTube by someone called Jim Rohn, an American motivational speaker and coach. He was one of the most successful motivational speakers in the world, and the video I watched was all about how changing your environment and the people you surrounded yourself with could change your life. Jim explained how removing toxic people from your life and surrounding yourself with positive people – people who were genuinely interested in your personal growth, rather than out for what they could get from you – could change the way you thought.

His words resonated with me so strongly that I watched the video again. Then I watched it a third time, and started taking notes. It felt as if Jim was speaking directly to me. I thought back over the recent months of excess. My old friends had seen my life fall apart, they had seen me on a spiral of self-destruction. But instead of trying to stop me, instead of reaching out a hand to help me, they had joined in for the fun of it. They had encouraged me to call my dealer, they had encouraged me to spend more and more money on alcohol, and then they had left me alone every time to face the comedown. My friends weren't to blame for what I did – I was. But now I could see that they had become part of the problem.

I started to realise that, like Jim had said, I had been surrounding myself with toxic people. Not just my friends, but the people I'd got to know who judged a person's worth solely on how much money they had and how many fast cars they owned. It was a degrading, harmful mindset, and one I had let myself be sucked into. Just like my friends, who had been jealous of my success, these people had not been interested in my personal growth – quite the opposite. They had made me feel I wasn't good enough, and when I had tried to better myself, they had done their best to undermine and belittle me.

I realised that what I needed was a complete change of environment. I needed to wipe the slate clean, to get away from the people and places that were dragging me into my self-hating, self-destructive lifestyle.

I had to admit the truth to my parents: that I had spent the last of my money on drink, drugs and girls. That even the pay-out from the house was gone now. That I had literally nothing left. After I took the last car back to the showroom and closed up the house, I moved back in with my parents. It was humiliating, as a grown man, to be living in my childhood bedroom, even though they welcomed me with open arms. Yet Jim's message had given me a spark of hope – something I hadn't felt for a very long time. The hope that a different kind of life might just be possible.

The first thing I needed to do, as Jim had said, was change my environment. I needed to be away from the surroundings that were toxic to me – somewhere far away from the pubs I frequented with my friends, the drug dealers I knew and the prostitutes I had on call. I found myself a flat miles away from my old house, in a new development where I knew absolutely no one. My local boozer was no longer round the corner, and the old temptations were out of reach.

You might think I'd feel more lonely stuck out there on my own, but the opposite was true. I loved the fact that I didn't know a soul. Not only was there no one to encourage me into my old patterns of behaviour, but no one around me knew about my past, my failed marriage and my spiral into drugs and alcohol. No one could judge me.

But moving away wasn't enough. I decided that if I was going to detox my life, I would have to cut off my old friends completely: to go no-contact with everyone from that former life who had contributed to how miserable I'd become.

That prospect scared the shit out of me. I'd always been a man's man, the kind of guy who liked hanging out in a pack. To extract myself from my friendship group of many years and go solo felt like jumping off the edge of a cliff. But I knew I had to do it. Sad as it was to let go of the past, and the history I had with these people, I also felt other emotions: anger and resentment. They had taken advantage of me when I was vulnerable. They hadn't been there for me when I needed them. And they had shown that they didn't respect me.

It was easier to put into practice than I thought. When friends who live near you can't be bothered to come round to check you're all right, they don't do it if you're 10 miles away. My friends tried calling me a few times, but when I didn't answer and didn't call them back, they soon gave up.

I had done it. I was friendless, and it was the best decision I'd ever made. It felt as if my life had been suddenly cleared, as if I'd been carrying a heavy weight on my back and had now simply put it down and found that I could walk with ease. All this time I had been carrying the baggage of bad relationships around without even realising the toll it was taking.

And by taking action, even though it was frightening, I

felt empowered. I realised I actually had control over what happened in my life. I could look honestly at what was and wasn't serving me, and I could choose to let go of the things that weren't. It was a powerful feeling.

Next, I had to find a new world to throw myself into, a more positive one than the world of money and materialism that I had been sucked into when I was married to Claire. I had always loved going to the gym, and I began to think that it could be the right workplace for me – a place where people went to better themselves, to get healthy and fit and achieve their own personal goals.

I was very lucky that my granddad gave me the money to get my license as a personal trainer, and I started working for a chain of gyms called Gymbox. The environment couldn't have been more different from the money-driven world of sales I had been used to. Everyone looked happy to be here, they came to de-stress rather than to get stressed. And the gym was a great leveller: everyone looks the same in a sweaty T-shirt and trainers, so it was impossible to tell who earned a six-figure salary and who didn't.

Before, I had always been frantically trying to score a higher and higher commission to fund my lavish lifestyle, and constantly worrying about the debts I was piling up. But here I had no motive when I came to work except to be happy and make other people happy. Every day, I woke up and told myself that that was my only goal.

Being in this new environment brought me into contact

with new kinds of people. Here were people who weren't doing drugs. Here were people who had good relationships with their partners. Here were people who were happy in their careers. They saved. They went on holiday with their families. They spent quality time with their loved ones. I looked at them and realised that this was real life. A healthy, happy kind of life, one that I could aspire to myself.

Over time, I began to build up true friendships with some of my clients, friendships that were not based on what they could get from me or what I could get from them. Having had so many toxic people in my life, I was extremely careful about who I chose to let into it now. If somebody started talking about what they had, or asked questions about what I had, I knew they were not for me. I wasn't interested in people who sat down and started a conversation about their new watch or car. I was interested in people who started talking about what they had learned recently. Who were on their own journey of personal growth, and were genuinely interested in mine.

One of these new kinds of people I came across was a guy called Mark. He was a very experienced paramedic, someone who had devoted his life to helping others. It was the opposite of all the people in my old life. I found I could really let my guard down with Mark, be honest and open up about the bad times I'd had. For the first time, I started telling someone outside my family about just how low I had sunk, how I'd been on my last legs and not known what to do with myself. How I'd lost all my money and lost my sense of self along the way, and how I was now trying to build up my identity from scratch.

Unlike my old 'friends', Mark was willing to listen, and he genuinely wanted to help. "Tim," he would say, when I was having a bad day, "you're doing so well now. Just look how far you've come. And look what you're doing for people in the gym – you're changing people's lives here."

I never felt judged by Mark for the mistakes I'd made, and I realised that that was what a true friend should be: someone who took you on face value and didn't judge you for your past.

Then there was a guy called Nick, a six foot tall ex-captain who was built like a tank. He was very well spoken, and on the surface we were like chalk and cheese. But as we got to know each other better I began to see that our values matched. He had an incredible energy about him, and he was honest and genuine. If something wasn't right he would tell you straight up, and I liked that about him. We began spending time together outside of personal training, doing podcasts together about the positive effect the gym could have on mental health.

Bit by bit, I was finding people whose values and ethos were in alignment with my own. Having spent so much time around the wrong people, I had far more clarity now when the right people came my way. But I would never have found those people if I had stayed in the environment I had been in before.

In order to make room for better relationships to come into your life, you first have to let go of the ones that are no longer serving you. I see it a bit like a wardrobe: if you want to fit new clothes in, you have to throw the old ones out. You have to make space for new friendships, in order to have the time and energy to invest in them.

And guess what? It turns out that in getting rid of one toxic person, you suddenly find you have the time and energy for 10 good ones.

'Dogs are not our whole life, but they make our lives whole.' Roger Caras

4

THE ART OF GRATITUDE, AND GIVING RATHER THAN TAKING

So I had a new flat and a new job, and I was starting to build a new life. On the outside, things were changing, and they were changing for the better.

But on the inside, I still had a long way to go. I couldn't help beating myself up mentally for what I'd done. When I thought back to all those coke and booze-filled nights and the meetings with prostitutes in the early hours – not to mention the money I'd got from the house sale that I had snorted up my nose – I felt so ashamed. I was no longer surrounded by the reminders of it – the empty bottles, the rolled-up bank notes, the filthy glasses in the sink – but inside my head, it was as if I hadn't completely cleared the evidence away.

Most of all, I felt terrible for having taken the decision that day to commit suicide. It seemed like the ultimate failure: the failure to even want to exist as a human being. And I felt guilty about the shock and trauma I had put my parents through by telling them what I had felt like doing. I still couldn't forget the look on my mother's face when she heard from her own son's lips that he hadn't wanted to live any more. Having worked so hard and sacrificed so much to give me everything she could when I was growing up, that must have been such a bitter blow for her.

All this internal judgement was going on inside my head every day when I got up in the morning to go to work. And even though I was now discovering a healthier way to live, and noticing more positive people coming into my life, part of me still didn't think I was good enough to be around those people, or strong enough to live a life like them. Sometimes, to blot out those negative thoughts, I would stay up late on my own in my new flat where nobody knew me, and drink a bit too much – which of course only led to me beating myself up more the following day.

The morning after one of those unhappy evenings, I hauled myself out of bed with a hangover and slumped on the sofa. I grabbed the remote, switched on the TV and started aimlessly channel hopping as I ate my breakfast.

I rubbed my bleary eyes as an advert came on for a charity appeal. It featured a little boy, somewhere in sub-Saharan Africa, starting *his* morning. He got up, walked many miles to a small river and collected water for his whole family. The water was filthy – contaminated with urine and faeces – but it was all there was, so he collected it and took it home.

As I watched this short film, I was jolted into reality. Here I was, lying on a comfortable sofa, in a comfortable flat, feeling sorry for myself. Yet there was no comparison between the day that l had to face and the day this kid had to face. The thought that he and his whole family would have to drink that dirty, contaminated water, not knowing whether it would keep them alive or kill them, was appalling. It made me feel sick. How could I carry on with my day as usual, knowing that this was happening to a young child somewhere in the world? I had to act.

I picked up the phone and dialled the number in the advert. I explained that I wanted to donate to the appeal I'd just seen on TV.

"Thank you, sir. How much would you like to donate?" the person on the other end asked. "£10? £50? £100?"

I didn't know. I honestly couldn't remember ever giving to charity before. In my old life, the one that had been all about money, I had never once thought about giving the stuff away. I had been 100% focused on what I could spend my money on for my own benefit – what pleasurable experiences I could buy with it, what material possessions I could acquire that would further my social status. I only looked at what I could get out of life, what life could give me, not what I could give back.

Ironically, it was only now, after I had been reduced to nothing and was struggling to make ends meet, that I had suddenly discovered the urge to help others. After the payments on my one-bed flat and other outgoings, I knew I only had about £300 left in my bank account to keep me going till the end of the month. But I also knew that my £300 could make so much more impact in the life of a child like the one I had seen in the advert than it possibly could to me. What was the worst that could happen? I might have to spend a bit less in the supermarket that week, but so what? Why couldn't I deprive myself a little bit, if it meant helping someone else so much?

"300," I said. "I'd like to donate £300."

I gave over my bank details and cleared my account in one go.

After I put the phone down, a strange thing happened to me. I felt euphoric. I had just given away the last penny I had, but instead of loss or regret I was feeling a sense of joy like nothing I'd ever experienced before. A strange, tingly feeling passed over my whole body, running down my spine and through my arms and legs. Could it be that giving was actually more of a high than taking?

In the days that followed I received texts from the charity, updating me on what my money was enabling them to do for children like the one I'd seen in the advert. I couldn't stop thinking about those kids, and soon I was reading more about the issues the charity worked on and setting up a monthly direct debit. For once in my life, I was thinking about things outside my own small sphere, asking what I could do for others rather than what I could get for myself.

But I did get something for myself, too. I got a release. A release from focusing on myself constantly, and on how badly I had messed up. After a few days, I realised I had been so busy thinking about the charity and those kids that the niggling thoughts about my old life, those judgemental, punishing thoughts, had grown a little quieter. In the grand scheme of things, in the vast scale of human existence, my problems were not so big after all. Compared to those kids, I was bloody lucky.

When I went to the gym that morning, the sense of being lucky went with me, and it changed my whole attitude. I smiled at everyone I encountered that day. I noticed every little thing that I had to be grateful for. I was grateful for the opportunity my granddad had given me to retrain and start afresh in a new career in personal training. I was grateful to the gym owner, who had given me a chance by hiring me. I was grateful to the clients who had booked with me, for putting their faith and trust in me and allowing me to help them. After everything I'd been through, after all the shameful things I'd done, I now had the chance to make something better of myself, and I was truly grateful for that.

I decided that, from now on, I was going to be someone who always tried to hold onto that sense of gratitude, even if I was having a bad day – because, let's face it, there's always someone, somewhere, whose day is so much worse than yours. I made sure I smiled and was friendly to everyone I saw at the gym, even when I was feeling low or full of regret. I decided they were all going to get the best version of me, because that was the version they deserved. And do you know what? It paid off. People started commenting on what a happy guy I was. They wanted to know: "Where do you get your energy from? How do you manage to be so positive all the time?" And the answer wasn't that I had more of anything than anyone else around me. It wasn't that I had some magic trick for creating instant happiness. It was simply that I had learned to appreciate what I'd got and be grateful. Just as my parents had done all those years before, because they'd come from nothing.

I still had my bad days, of course – everyone does. But now I made practising gratitude part of my regular routine, a technique I learned from the coaching videos I had watched. Every morning, straight after waking, I got out a notebook and pen, set a timer for 15 minutes, and just wrote down every single thing I had to be grateful for.

I started by taking a deep breath in, and then breathing out. Because when you strip it all back, the first thing we can all be grateful for is our breath, the thing that keeps us alive. Sometimes I would think about the day I almost killed myself, and how that could easily have been my last breath. Instead I was here, still breathing, and that was the first, most basic thing I had to be grateful for.

Then I would think about how grateful I was to have a healthy, functioning body that allowed me to do the things I was doing: going to the gym, helping people train. I would think about how grateful I was for the delicious coffee that I was going to have at breakfast that morning before work, and how grateful I was that I didn't have to walk 10 miles to get clean water to drink. How grateful I was for the beautiful day outside the window and the sun that was shining and the hours I had ahead of me to do the things I loved. I would think about how grateful I was for the clients I knew I was going to see that day and how much they inspired me, just as they now said I inspired them.

After 15 minutes, I would close the notebook and put it in a drawer. I never read what I'd written once I'd done it, but the effect that writing it had on me lasted the rest of the day. It made me feel grounded. It reminded me what was important in life, and what wasn't. It brought me back into the present and stopped me ruminating on the past and the things I felt ashamed of, the things that I couldn't change. It reminded me of the wonderful opportunities that lay ahead and the things I felt inspired to do. It set me up for the day with a positive mindset and helped me be the best version of myself that I could be.

If you've never thought of keeping a gratitude diary before, I don't blame you. If someone had told me to do it in the past, I would have laughed in their face. The old me only felt grateful for the sound my Aston Martin made when I turned the key in the ignition. But I'm telling you, give it a try. Because no matter where you are in your life, or how bad things have got, realising how much you already have to be thankful for is a gift.

Seeing that advert on TV and giving my last penny to charity was a big turning point in my life. After that, I started asking myself what more I could do to help people who were worse off than I was. Alongside my work at the gym, I started running fitness boot camps and donating a quarter of the profits to cancer research. I brought the clients I knew from the gym on board, they told all their friends, and soon it was pretty successful, making a decent amount of money for charity every month. I also started doing work for Pencils for Promise, an organisation that builds schools in developing countries.

To my surprise, the more time I devoted to charity and to thinking about others rather than myself, the happier I became – and the more I realised how spiritually bankrupt my old life had been. I had thought that being able to buy all the expensive things that I hadn't been able to afford when I was growing up would make me feel happy and fulfilled. I had devoted my life to making money to acquire all those things. But ironically, the more I had bought, the less happy I had become. Yes, I'd experienced a quick rush to the head when I drove a brand spanking new sports car out of the showroom, or strapped on my latest designer watch. It had been relatively easy to get that short-term ego boost just by flexing my credit card. But each time I did it, the sense of excitement had quickly faded, leaving me wanting a newer, faster car or an even fancier watch. They were just quick fixes – sticking plasters. There was no longevity with that kind of happiness.

By contrast, the kind of happiness I experienced when I raised money towards building a school in Africa or fighting cancer was an enduring kind of happiness. It was about doing something for the long term, leaving a legacy, contributing to something bigger than my own existence. I had found something that I valued more than myself, and ironically that made me feel good. Soon I was hooked on this new kind of thrill: the thrill of doing things for other people.

I was now on the lookout constantly for more causes I could get involved with. One day I decided to watch a documentary about Great Ormond Street Hospital and was shocked to learn that many of the parents of children at the hospital couldn't afford to stay in London to be with them while they had major surgery. Christmas was approaching, and while everyone else was at home enjoying themselves with their families these kids were going to be on their own, dealing with some of the hardest experiences of their lives. I felt compelled to do something to make that time a little bit easier for them. I thought that if I could somehow raise enough money to buy toys for all the kids then that would at least go some way towards helping.

The gym was the obvious place to start. I put the word around that I intended to do a sponsored indoor rowing challenge and asked if anyone would like to join me. Soon I had seven other people keen to be on my team, and we decided to set ourselves a target of 100,000 metres in relay. I knew it would be a gruelling challenge, and probably take all day, but if we were going to do it then I wanted to do it big. The plan was to use all the money to go to Toys R Us afterwards and buy an enormous haul of presents that we could take up to the hospital for Christmas.

When we told everyone at the gym what we were doing, the response was amazing. I set up a JustGiving page and was touched by how many of my clients and their friends were willing to dig deep to support the cause. The time of year and the fact that everyone was getting into the Christmas spirit didn't hurt.

I was doing my best to promote the event all over social media, and one day a guy reached out to me personally on Facebook to say how close the appeal was to his own heart. His little girl was in Great Ormond Street Hospital right now, he explained, and she was fighting for her life. Getting these toys would make such a difference to her and to all the other kids on the ward who were going through a difficult time.

Hearing his personal story made me feel even more committed to the challenge, and I asked if he would be willing to come round and do a Facebook Live video with me all about what we were doing. Talking live on the internet was totally out of my comfort zone, but I was so committed now that I knew I had to do it.

The video turned out to be the best piece of publicity we could possibly have had, and with the little girl's dad telling his story it was incredibly powerful. The film went viral, and suddenly we had 10,000 views. My JustGiving page went crazy and we hit £6,000 and counting.

This idea of mine was really gaining momentum, and every day now I woke up buzzing with excitement. But then I started to think maybe it was all just a bit too easy. Was I really pushing myself hard enough? OK, so we were rowing 100,000 metres, and maybe I'd get some pulled muscles, but what was that compared to what those kids were going through in hospital? Some of them were dying of cancer – this could be their last Christmas. I had to do more.

The night before the challenge, I did a new Facebook Live video and announced to my whole team that I was doubling the distance. We would now be rowing 200,000 metres.

The following morning, I woke up and wrote on my whiteboard: *Today's the day.* I knew the challenge I'd set for myself was going to be tough, but I also knew that the thought of those sick kids would get me through.

The gym was packed, and as we started rowing everyone cheered. My team and I took it in turns to row 500 metres each, high-fiving each other as we came off the machine. In between stints we each went around with a bucket, collecting change to keep the money rolling in right up till the last minute.

Throughout the day, people dropped in whenever they could to provide moral support, including many of my clients who had got behind the idea from the start. All the way through we had someone with a video camera filming the event for social media and interviewing all the rowers whenever they took breaks.

A few hours in, I realised what a gruelling challenge we'd set ourselves, and when I looked at my team members I realised how exhausted they were. But all of us were so hyped by the support we were getting, both in the gym and online, and so committed to the cause of helping the children at Great Ormond Street, that I knew there was no way any of us were going to give up.

Almost six hours later we were finally down to the last 2,000 metres, and I was determined to do the final stretch myself. I had started this insane venture, and now I knew it had to be me that ended it. I climbed into the machine and started rowing, my body already so knackered from a whole day of rowing that I could feel it groaning as I pulled on the oars again. Somehow I got through the first 1,500 metres without too much trouble, but on the last 500 I truly felt like I was going to die. My whole body was in pain, and my glutes and hamstrings felt like they were on fire. I was sick to my stomach and breathing far too fast.

As I reached the last few metres my vision was going blurry and I thought I was going to pass out. But then I heard the crowd around me beginning to chant: "Tim! Tim! Tim!" Their shouts pulled me back from the brink and spurred me on, forcing me to keep going through the physical pain I was experiencing. I knew they were chanting for my rowing, but to me, it felt like so much more. It felt like they were chanting for my soul, like they were behind me in this new journey I was on in my life, and they were supporting the enormous change I was making.

When I hit 200,000 metres the crowd erupted into cheers and applause. I fell off the machine, rolled onto the floor and immediately vomited everywhere. Everyone rushed over to help, putting my legs up in the air to try and get rid of the lactic acid. My face was bright purple and tears were running down my cheeks. I was a complete and utter wreck, both physically and emotionally.

But I had never felt stronger than I did in that moment. I had proved that I could literally come back from the dead; that from being someone who felt so bad about themselves they wanted to end it all, I had discovered an inner strength that I had never known existed. Finally, after months of unsteady progress, always doubting whether I really had it in me to change and build a new life for myself, I had come back fighting. And I knew that this was only the beginning for me.

Once all the rowers had had a group hug and popped a bottle of champagne, I got out my mobile, retreated to a quiet corner and called my mum.

"Mum, I did it," I said. "And I'm ready to start a new life now."

'You gain strength, courage and confidence by every experience in which you really stop to look fear in the face. You are able to say to yourself, "I lived through this horror. I can take the next thing that comes along."' Eleanor Roosevelt

5

WORKING OUT WHAT YOU REALLY WANT AND LEARNING TO TAKE ACTION

The Value of Coaching

That rowing challenge was a life-changing experience for me. In pushing myself to the brink, in almost killing myself on that machine, it was as if I had been reborn. That moment was the death of the old Tim Cooper – the one who had drifted so far away from his true values, whose life had come crashing down around him so spectacularly, and who didn't think he deserved anything better. I had shown myself that actually I had an amazing amount of resilience. If I could come back from near-death to achieve something so positive, I could do anything.

In helping others, I had also found a real sense of meaning and fulfilment in a way I had never thought possible before. From thinking about how I could give to charities and people I had never met, soon I was starting to look at how I could take that ethos and apply it to my daily life and the people around me. I found myself having different kinds of conversations with people than I had had before. In my old life, conversations had all been about what I had been spending my money on – the expensive holidays I'd been on or the five-star restaurants I'd eaten at. But now I wanted to have deeper conversations with the people I came into contact with. I wanted to find out about what really made them tick. I wanted to know if they felt unfulfilled, and if they did, I wanted to help them and show them what I had discovered – that a more fulfilling life was possible.

During my training sessions with my clients, increasingly we were spending as much time talking as we were working out. We would be having conversations about their life goals, not just their fitness goals. We would be discussing why they wanted to get in shape, not just how they were going to do it. We discussed what they really wanted from life, not just what they wanted from their workout. The more I took an interest in people and listened to them, the more I found they opened up and confided in me in return.

But there was a problem with this. I was trying to help people find their purpose in life, and that was not what a personal trainer was meant to be doing. I was meant to be encouraging my clients to lift a 100kg barbell – and ideally filming it, to show off the fact that they had done it. I was meant to be working on their bodies, not their minds. I was beginning to realise that there was a fundamental disconnect between the ethos of personal training and the person that I was becoming. I knew I was a good personal trainer, but for that reason I was never going to be the best. Things were heading in the right direction for me, but I was still confused about where my true path in life lay.

One day, I was working in the gym when a guy I'd not seen before came in. We started chatting, and I immediately liked his energy. There was something about him that drew me to him. I asked him what he did for a living.

"Oh, I'm a lifestyle coach," he replied.

"A what?"

"A lifestyle coach. I help people work out what they really want in life and help them achieve it."

I was amazed. I'd been listening to coaches like Jim Rohn for months on the internet, but I had never met one in real life.

Over the next few days I kept seeing this guy in the gym, and I kept being struck by his incredible energy. I knew I wanted to find out more, so one day I asked him how much it would cost to book a session with him.

"Well, how about we have a coffee first and a chat?" he replied.

Over coffee, he started asking me questions. A lot of questions. *What kind of person are you? What's the most important thing to you? What are your values? Are you being true to who you are right now?* They were the kind of questions I needed, the questions I had to answer if I was ever to discover my true path in life. I knew I could have gone for counselling or psychotherapy to help me figure things out, but they had never appealed to me. They seemed to be all about raking over the past and what had gone wrong – and if I knew one thing, it was that I was done with the past. I was over it. I wanted to move on.

By contrast, lifestyle coaching seemed to be focused on the present and the future – on working out the gap between where I was now and where I wanted to be, and working out how to close that gap. It was about coming up with a plan and getting results relatively quickly, not spending years and years lying on a couch.

By the end of the coffee, I had signed up for a three-month stint of lifestyle coaching. It wasn't cheap – in fact, it was pretty expensive – but I felt it was money well spent. It wasn't about buying something that would soon lose its shine. It was about investing in myself for the long term.

To pay for the sessions I worked extra hard in the gym, taking on more clients and pulling long shifts. Despite my wobbles about personal training I threw myself into what I was doing and soon became known as 'Tim in the Gym', because I was there so much. But I knew I had to find the money to pay for the coaching. It had become my mission.

The first thing I did with my lifestyle coach was to really pin down what my own values were and what was important to me. It did mean thinking back over my past life to some extent, but rather than trawling through the bad times and attempting to analyse them, the focus was on pinpointing the good stuff – the positive moments, the times when I felt most like myself. I asked myself who I really was and what I really stood for, once all the noise and clutter was removed. Who was the most authentic Tim Cooper, representing the values that I most wanted to live by? And what were the thought patterns that had prevented that version of myself from coming to the fore?

When it came to it, I realised, striving to be rich for its own sake was not who I was. I had been brought up to value the simple things in life and to be grateful for what I had. I was someone who actually valued close relationships and family over and above material things. Somehow, somewhere along the line, I had lost touch with that. Part of what I needed to work on was how not to be influenced by people who had a different agenda. I had to learn how to hold on to my values and principles and not be swayed so easily by outside influences, whether that was my social circle or social media. I had to learn to have faith in my own beliefs and trust my gut instincts more. So many aspects of the toxic life I had lived before had not sat well with me deep down, yet I had tuned out from my inner voice. Now I learned that I could get back in touch with it and trust it to tell me what I really needed.

I asked myself what the positive qualities were that made me who I was. What would people who truly loved me and cared about me say that they admired about me? These were not questions I would have dared ask myself before, having felt so ashamed of the unhappiness I had caused my parents. But

I realised that there *were* good parts to my character – some that had even come out of the crisis I had recently faced. For a start, I had shown bravery. Bravery in choosing not to give up when I was on the verge of suicide. Bravery in opening up and being honest with my family about how low I was feeling. And bravery in cutting off all my old so-called friends, moving to a new area and starting a brand-new life on my own. It hadn't been easy, but I had done it.

I had also shown resourcefulness in working out what skills and experiences I had that I could use to launch myself into a new career and build up what was now a successful personal training business from scratch. And above all, I had shown a remarkable level of resilience: I had bounced back from so many setbacks and such a state of despair, and was now discovering a new sense of purpose and happiness through the positive things I was doing for others.

When I looked at myself through this new lens, I could see that I was someone with unique qualities that could empower me and enable me to achieve even more in the future. I realised that I was actually a very entrepreneurial person, someone who was suited to working on their own initiative and running their own business, and that this was something I felt driven to do. My qualities of bravery, resourcefulness and resilience were all assets that I could draw on to make this a reality.

But I needed to work out where to invest my skills and time. I had been putting all my energy into my role at the gym, and it had served its purpose: it had got me out of a hole when

I needed money and provided an escape route from my old life. Aspects of it had proved to be very positive, and generally it was a healthier environment than my old job in sales. But over time I had come to realise that the ethos of the gym – of working on the external rather than the internal – was not a good fit for me. Now that I was more in touch with my values, I knew I was someone who cherished human relationships over material things, who craved deeper, more meaningful connections with others. I liked working with people, but I could see that a different kind of relationship with clients was what I needed.

I asked myself, *What do you naturally find yourself doing? What are the roles you tend to fall into in your relationships with other people? What things do you find yourself gravitating towards, over and over again, that make you feel happy?* The answer was staring me in the face: it was helping other people, the way that my lifestyle coach was helping me. Without it having been a conscious decision, increasingly the conversations I was having with my clients were all about helping them on their journeys, finding out what was making them feel stuck, blocked, unhappy – and trying to help them work out how to achieve the life they really wanted. Having suffered so much myself, I now had a burning desire to stop suffering in whatever form, whether that was the child starving in Africa or the ordinary man or woman walking down the street who felt lost in their life.

The next time I saw my lifestyle coach, I told him, "I want

to do what you do."

"Tim," he said, "I'll never forget when we first met and I told you I was a lifestyle coach. Your eyes lit up like saucers."

I realised it was true. Part of what had drawn me to him was not just that I needed help myself, but that I saw in him what I could become. But I'd had to realise something about myself first: I'd had to realise that the problems I'd faced, far from making me weak and unfit to help others, had actually made me stronger and more able to empathise with those who were also going through a tough time. Not only that, but they could act as an inspiration to people who felt they had no way out, who felt their lives were unsalvageable, as I had done. I had shown myself and could now show others that there was always a way to turn your life around, that there was always hope. And I could help them find that inner strength and resilience that they didn't believe they had, but that all of us have inside, and that we can all draw on.

Working out what I really wanted to do with my life and how to live in tune with my values was the first part of the process with my lifestyle coach. The next step was building my belief in myself and my determination to get there, and mapping out how I would do it. It was then that I learned about the power of visualisation.

I didn't just tell myself that I wanted to be a lifestyle coach: I saw it. I saw myself sitting with clients, talking to them and guiding them. And more than that, I realised I wanted to help more people, on a bigger scale. So I visualised myself in a massive auditorium, with thousands of people listening to what I said and being helped by it. Then, I drew it out. Yes, I actually got a pen and paper and drew a picture of myself in that auditorium. I drew the microphone, I drew the audience. It was another one of those exercises that my old self would have baulked at, but that picture helped me so much. It gave me an image of my dream life, which I could look at whenever I needed to remind myself where I was going. And by getting it down on paper, it felt like it had form. It was no longer a vague, nebulous wish in my mind but a real place and time that I was travelling towards.

Then we worked out what steps I needed to take to get to that place, and I committed to taking action every single day to get me closer to it. I took courses in lifestyle coaching, neuro-linguistic programming and counselling. I set a deadline for leaving my work at the gym and launching myself in my new career. This wasn't what I had instinctively thought of doing – my first thought had been to become an online coach first and continue the personal training – but my lifestyle coach gave me the push I needed. He made me see that to give myself the best shot, I had to put my all into this new venture and accept the initial financial hit.

It was this sense of structure and a clear plan that lifestyle coaching gave me. It had first helped me crystallise what it was I really craved, and now it was getting me on track to actually make it happen. Without it, I might have spent years procrastinating and putting off the decision to make that change.

As it happened, I left the gym a month and a half before my self-imposed deadline – and my first client came to me. I was working out in a private gym in west London one day and got chatting to the owner, who asked what I did for a living. "I'm a lifestyle coach," I told him, without thinking. I explained how I could help people who were struggling to find their way in life and show them how to change their mindset. The owner was very interested and asked me to come and give a talk about it at the opening of his new gym.

I went along and gave a seminar all about my own personal experiences, and how lifestyle coaching had changed everything for me. I told them how I was now passionate about doing the same for others who were feeling lost or in crisis, for whatever reason that might be. The talk went down very well, and not long afterwards I got a call from the gym owner.

"Tim," he said, "there's someone I'd like you to meet. He's a friend of mine, and he's in a really bad place. We've tried everything."

The friend in question was a very young man who I'll call 'Bill'. Bill had lost his way in life: he was jobless, living off his dad and spending most of his time in his bedroom. He had become increasingly anxious, which showed itself in the way he constantly scratched himself. He wasn't eating properly and his room was always a mess.

I met Bill at a station in west London, and when I first saw him he was scratching like crazy. "Well done for coming to meet me," I told him. "I know how tough it must have been."

He nodded.

"So," I said. "You're feeling anxious. How about we start by standing up and doing some public speaking in the station?"

He looked at me quickly, then realised I was joking.

"I'm just being silly," I assured him, "but by the end of this you'll be able to do it."

I'd broken the ice, and soon Bill was talking to me. He talked to me because I spoke to him like a normal person – a friend – unlike many of the professionals he'd been sent to before. He'd closed down with everyone else, feeling that they were trying to delve into his mind and look back over what had happened in his past. No one had asked him what he wanted for his future.

I noticed that Bill was wearing camouflage bottoms, and I asked him about them. He told me that he was into paintball, but that it was something he'd stopped doing. He told me about other things he liked doing – problem solving, working as part of a team – all things that he had stopped doing since he'd lost his confidence.

At the end of our first session, I put my arm around Bill. "This is just the beginning," I told him. "We are going to crush this."

Bill turned to go, but then he stopped. "I've got to say before I go," he said, "that this is the best I've felt in months. The thing about you, Tim, is I can tell that you actually give a shit."

Over the following weeks, Bill and I mapped out what he

really wanted in life. We did a vision board, just as I had done, getting him to draw what his dreams looked like on a piece of paper. We worked out what was really important to him, and bit by bit, step by baby step, we got there.

We cleared out the habits and behaviours that weren't serving him anymore, and we replaced them with new ones. We gave him structure. I demanded photos to prove that he was tidying his room. Photos of him applying for jobs. Photos of him going out for walks in the fresh air and eating proper food. Yes, he was accountable to me, to begin with at least, but the point was that I was putting into place new habits and behaviours, and after a while Bill didn't need me to police him anymore. He had discovered for himself which things were serving him and which weren't.

Soon Bill had a driving license. He had a girlfriend. He had a job in marketing and he was playing paintball with his friends again. In short, his life had totally changed. And guess what? The scratching had stopped.

When I first met Bill, I asked him to write the word 'hope' down on a piece of paper, telling him it represented how much positivity he felt about his future. He wrote it in tiny letters that were almost unreadable. Three weeks later, I asked him to write it again, and it was a little bit bigger. A couple of months down the line, those letters were capital letters, and they filled up the entire page.

Soon, I found the life-coaching just snowballed. Once word got out about what I did, more and more people came out of the woodwork and I didn't even have to advertise. There was 'Len', a man with lots of letters after his name, who did endless courses to improve his qualifications but never took any action. Years of bullying by his father had made him so self-critical that he never took any risks. By the time I went to see him, he was ready to break down. He'd had enough.

I helped Len let go of the past and start grabbing his future. I made him visualise what he wanted and work out how to get it. Soon he was designing a new online business platform that was going to change his whole industry. He believed in himself more and was less judgemental towards himself and other people.

Next came a young woman from a very wealthy family whose parents were tearing their hair out because she lay in bed every day till 11am doing nothing. She had lost all motivation in life and had no idea how to stand on her own two feet. Soon I had her setting up her own website for her work as a make-up artist; she started getting bookings and styling people for photoshoots. She discovered that when she took action, motivation followed – and that she was more than capable of breaking away from her parents and fending for herself.

Then there was the fashion PA who had studied design at university, but whose life had come crashing down after her sister died of cancer and her father lost all his money and hit the bottle. Through it all, she'd been everyone's rock, supporting them all, and now these experiences were making her reassess her chosen career. She realised that the world of fashion didn't sit well with her values, and that what she really wanted to do was to make a difference in people's lives. Now she's developing programmes to help people with loss, anxiety, stress and relationship breakdowns, and she feels she's found her calling.

With each person I coach, I spend time pinning down what their priorities are in life, and what really matters to them. Then I ask them whether they're living in accordance with those priorities. So many people find they're living a life that's a shadow of the life they truly want to lead. They've found themselves going down a path that someone else has carved out for them, or they've taken the easy route once too often because they're scared to take a risk or really test themselves. They need to get back in touch with who they were truly meant to be, and the life they dreamed of having before the negative thought patterns got in the way. They need to be shown that they really can achieve that life, that it's theirs for the taking, with the right plan.

And that, for me, is the value of a lifestyle coach. Coaching removes all the clutter: the bad habits that have built up over the years, the negative self-talk, the expectations of other people and the baggage of regret. It cuts through all that and gets back to the fundamentals.

If you need your teeth checked, you call a dentist. If your pipes are leaking, you call a plumber. But if your life's heading in the wrong direction and you know it, my advice to you is: call a lifestyle coach.

'You build on failure. You use it as a stepping stone. Close the door on the past. You don't try to forget the mistakes, but you don't dwell on it. You don't let it have any of your energy, or any of your time, or any of your space.' *Johnny Cash*

6

WORK ISN'T EVERYTHING

Learning to Lead a Balanced Life

I was working full time now as a lifestyle coach, and I had finally found my passion. Not only that, but it was becoming a successful business, turning over more than my personal training ever had. So many of my clients were people who, like me, needed help finding their calling. This often – but not always – related to their career choices and ambitions.

Yet the more I worked with people, the more I found that work was only part of the bigger picture of why people were unhappy. One of my clients, 'Matt', was extremely successful in his career, but had totally lost touch with other things in his life that were important – in particular, his relationship with his girlfriend. Matt worked long hours, and when he finally came home, 'Lara' would be waiting for him with a glass of wine, looking forward to having a nice dinner together. But the smartphone came to the dinner table with him, and instead of really giving his attention to her, he was effectively still working: checking emails, responding to messages. They very rarely had quality time together, because Matt was always too busy.

The first thing we looked at was how we could carve out more time to invest in the other areas of Matt's life. He felt he didn't have any more hours in the day, and that it just wasn't possible. But one thing Matt did have a lot of was money. We decided to use that money to get him a chauffeur, so that he could spend his journeys to and from the office working and could then afford to take time off in the evening to spend with Lara. The phone was banned at the dinner table, and they started spending the meal talking to each other.

Then we looked at why Matt and Lara were not spending quality time together. The key was planning. Without planning time in for trips and nights out with Lara, inevitably work and work-related engagements ate up all of Matt's spare time. I made him get into the habit of getting his diary out and booking in a three-hour slot to spend time with his girlfriend, even if it was two weeks in advance. Planning so far ahead might sound unromantic, but it was a game changer in their relationship.

These days, my approach to coaching is to map out people's lives across eight distinct areas – and work and career are only one. The others are family and friends; health and fitness; personal development and growth; physical environment; money and finance; love and romance; and fun and joy. These eight areas are the key things that need to be worked on to achieve real, lasting happiness, and even if a person is flying high in one area, if they are neglecting any of the others, they will not feel fulfilled.

I map out with my clients where they're at in each area of their life right now; often when we draw it out, it's immediately obvious where the imbalance lies. Typically, they're putting everything into work, or family responsibilities, and very little into investing in themselves, or finding time for fun and joy. Then we look at what things they'd like to be doing in their ideal life, in each area, and work out how to make these things happen. Frequently, as with Matt, they tell me it just isn't possible, that they don't have time. But so often the reality is simply that their *habits* need changing. They have got into the habit of spending their time one way, and have forgotten that they have a choice, that things really can be done differently. And of course, new habits take time and effort to instil; they don't just happen overnight. As a coach, I'm their cheerleader – but also for a while their sergeant major, pushing them to keep going with those new habits, even on the days when they don't feel like it.

I learned the hard way about the need for balance, and for making life about more than just work. My first ever job was selling high-end hair products to salons. After growing up in a cash-strapped household, having my own money coming in at last felt amazing. For the first time in my life I could afford to buy a small car, and the sense of independence and freedom was incredible. I was determined to hang onto that job and make the sales manager proud.

My approach to making sales was unstoppable. I got up at 6am every day and kept knocking on salon doors until every hairdresser in town had gone home for the night, often returning well after 9pm. I went out in rainstorms, I went out when it snowed. I went out when the weather was so bad that all the other sales guys stayed in the office. I knew those were the best times to catch the salon owners, because they'd be staying indoors too. When one of my colleagues boasted that he'd opened eight accounts that day, I replied that I'd opened 16. And that wasn't even one of my best days.

I had wanted to impress my boss, and of course it worked. Who wouldn't want an employee so dedicated to the job? All I heard was how great my results were, how outstanding my feedback from clients was. The praise and affirmation was intoxicating, the sense of success addictive. I wanted more.

Buoyed by my good feedback, and with a few thousand pounds in the bank from all the commission I'd made, I decided to set up on my own. The job in sales had shown me that I had energy, initiative and an entrepreneurial spirit, and now I wanted to take those things and make them work for me.

Since I knew the hairdressing industry, I decided to start there. I saw a gap in the market for a really high-quality magazine that rated salons, along the lines of the *Michelin Guide*. I called it *The Salon Bible* and got the best graphic designers in London, who worked on *GQ* and *FHM*, to design it for me. This was going to be a top-quality glossy that every salon would want to feature in. The idea was to start with 10,000 copies, hand-delivered to A- and B-graded households in my area, with plans to expand distribution after the first issue.

Once I was working for myself, on my own project, my work ethic went beyond unstoppable. It was turbo charged. Now I was getting up at 5am, drawing up my call sheet for the day and heading out early so I was ready to knock on salons as soon as they opened in the morning. I ran my appointments back to back, running into one salon to talk to them about the magazine, before rushing back to my car and driving to the next. When I got home in the evenings, I would write up all the copy for the magazine, upload all the pictures I had taken and send it off to the designers. Then when the pages came back I would proofread and edit them late into the night, before starting all over again with my salon visits the following day. In short, I was the researcher, the writer, the photographer, the editor and the salesman for this publication. I was doing everything myself. I was a one-man band.

Once again, it looked like my crazy work schedule was paying off. My outgoings for the first issue were £8,000, but I was on track to bring in £30,000 in revenue. I was going to profit by £22,000 per issue! I was going to be a big success.

My hard work was paying off on my balance sheet, but what I didn't stop to notice was how badly out of balance the rest of my life was. My crazy schedule didn't leave time for anything but work. It didn't leave time for friends and family. It didn't leave time for having fun. It didn't leave time for working out and staying fit. Hell, it didn't even leave time to eat on a lot of days – and if it did, it was fast food that I guzzled in between appointments so that I could keep going.

And one day, out of the blue, I couldn't keep going any more. I went to get up in the morning, and my body just wouldn't do it. My arms and legs didn't work. My body had shut down.

Why had it shut down? Because I wasn't feeding it. I wasn't giving it enough calories. I wasn't giving it enough vitamins and minerals. I wasn't giving it enough rest. I was so stressed over the enormous task I had given myself that stress hormones were flooding my body and crippling it.

I rang my mum, and she came over straight away.

"Oh my god Tim," she said, when she saw me. "What have you done to yourself? You're working too hard. You've got to stop."

"I can't," I replied. "I've put everything into this magazine and it launches in two weeks' time. I have to carry on."

"You can't Tim. Look at the state of you!"

She was right, of course. I was bed bound. All I could do was lie there, as day after day my mum took care of me and tried to feed me up again.

It wasn't just that my body had collapsed. My immune system was shot to pieces too. A tiny pimple on the top of my leg, which had started off looking like an ingrowing hair, had suddenly grown in size and turned violet around the edges. It was throbbing with pain.

When I woke up the next day, my right leg had completely seized up and the lower half of it was drained of colour. The pimple was now an abscess the size of a tennis ball, and there was a second one on my calf that was the size of a golf ball. I tried to get out of bed, but as soon as I put weight on the leg I screamed in pain.

"I've got to go to hospital," I told my mum. Finally, I had admitted that I wasn't well.

My mum drove me to Princess Alexandra Hospital and I put my arm around her shoulder and limped into Casualty.

The doctor examining me looked worried. "We need to make an incision and drain this immediately," he said, "otherwise your leg is at risk."

As the words sank in, I realised how seriously I had gambled with my health. Here I was, a young man in his 20s, who had been fit and healthy just a few months ago. Now I was lying on a hospital bed, facing the possibility of having my leg amputated.

The doctor went away and came back with a scalpel and a freezing spray to numb my leg. He began spraying the area round the larger abscess. Then the spray stopped.

"Oh, it's run out," he said. "I'll just go and get some more."

A few minutes later he returned. "I'm so sorry, but the whole hospital has run out," he told me. There was nothing for it: I would have to be cut open as I was.

When the doctor inserted the scalpel, I screamed blue murder – very blue.

"Can you keep your language down, please?" he said.

But worse was to come. Once he had made the incision, the doctor had to get either side of the abscess and push out the infection from deep within my flesh. When he put his fingers on each side and applied pressure, at first just a little bit of blood trickled out – but then suddenly a huge gushing torrent of yellow puss spurted out all over me and all over the floor. Even in my agony I couldn't believe how much there was.

But the doctor still wasn't convinced it had all come out, and in the end I had to have surgery. They had to dig four inches into my flesh to get that tennis ball-sized lump out, and two and a half inches for the other one. It took four metres of gauze to pack the holes that were left behind.

A few days later, as I lay recovering in hospital, my mum came to visit and said she had something to show me. She opened her bag and brought out a magazine – my magazine. It had just come back from the printers.

I took it in one shaky hand and looked at it. Here it was, my dream, in front of me. And here I was, lying helpless in a hospital bed, unable to get it delivered. The money I had made on advertising I would now have to use to live on for the next few months while I recuperated. I would not be able to pay for the delivery, nor would I be able to fund the next edition. Some friends helped by delivering a few hundred copies, but it was nowhere close to the 10,000 I had promised. And as a result, I had lots of angry advertisers to deal with, who I would have to pay back in instalments for months to come.

As I held that magazine in my hand, I broke down completely. I was devastated. I had worked so hard to be a success that I had caused my own failure. My dream was in tatters, and so too now was my health. By putting everything into one area – work – I had completely neglected every other aspect of my life, and ironically it had made me unable to work at all. My lifestyle had become toxic, and in the end it had poisoned me.

And worst of all, the experience had served only to convince me that I wasn't cut out to be a success. There were people out there who were just good at doing things, and I wasn't one of them. I just didn't have it in me to do the thing that I was drawn to: being an entrepreneur, doing something I felt passionate about and running my own business. I told myself that I was destined to work for someone else, to be number two or three in a business and no more. So when I got back up from my bed I got my head down and went to work in sales again.

It took the intervention of my lifestyle coach, years later, to really unpick those negative, self-limiting thoughts. That judgemental mindset that told me that what had happened was proof that I wasn't good enough, that told me it was better not to try than to try and risk failure. But from talking to him, I learned a few things. I learned that each perceived failure is a step on the path to success. And that by trying and failing, I had already achieved a lot more than the thousands of people who don't ever try, but live a safe and unfulfilled life on the side lines.

Now, I ask myself, *If this doesn't work out, what will I have got out of it?* I got a lot out of my 'failure'. I learned that I needed to do things because they mattered to me and I really cared about them for their own sake, not to prove myself to other people. I learned that the only people who mattered were the ones who loved me for who I was, and that they weren't judging me anyway. And most of all I learned to change my idea of what success looked like – away from one that was all about external affirmation and towards one that was about internal happiness and fulfilment.

My perceived 'failure' provided me with some very important lessons in a practical sense, too. I realised that in future I needed to work smarter, not harder. Working hard is running a business from inside it. Working smart is running a business from the outside. It's the difference between standing at the top of the mountain, seeing everything that's going on in the valley, and being in the valley, running around in the middle of all the chaos. Now, I employ people to run around in the valley, and I get on with what I'm good at: leading the business and helping my clients with their lives. Rather than being a one-man band, driving myself into the ground by trying to do everything on my own, I have learned to delegate.

Someone who's good at social media does my social media. Someone who's good at program design and content does my program design and content. Someone who's good at admin does all my invoices. That leaves me to focus on the things I actually feel passionate about doing. It was tough at first, because part of the problem was the feeling that I had to be in control of everything. But if I was sitting there for three hours a day doing paperwork that would dramatically reduce the amount of time I could spend with clients, and that's the whole point of my business.

When I looked back at what I had tried to do with the magazine, I could see that it had been unsustainable because I just hadn't had enough hands on deck: I had needed at least three other people working on that project alongside me. But it was also unsustainable because of the goals I set myself. I tried to do too much too quickly, and that put a terrible pressure on me that ultimately led to me getting ill. Most people overestimate what they can do in six months and underestimate what they can do in two years. My ethos now is to under promise and over deliver. That's why I only work with a set number of clients, rather than taking on as many as I can. I'd rather invest properly in those few clients than stretch myself too thin.

But the biggest lesson I learned was that work isn't everything. Most people, whether they realise it or not, make work and career their number one priority. It's an easy trap to fall into, especially when you spend the majority of each day working. But just because you spend the most time on it, that doesn't mean it's the most important thing in your life. If this was your last day on earth, what would you do? Would you go to the office? No. You'd be spending it doing the things you love, with the people you love. Now, I prioritise my family and friends and my health and fitness above my work and career. That's a big change for someone who felt achieving things at work was the be all and end all.

But above all else, my number one priority now is me. That might sound selfish, but let me explain. If I don't invest in me, in doing things I need to do to feel well and grounded, then I'm not able to be my best self around the people I love. I'm too tired to exercise, and I won't perform well at work. That's why I now start every day investing in myself, in my state of mind. It's partly about writing my gratitude diary, as I explained earlier, but it's also about doing other things that calm me, that feed me. I still get up early every day, but now instead of rushing headlong into work and other responsibilities, I meditate for 15 minutes. That brings me back into the moment. It reminds me to slow down and retain a sense of balance, no matter what the day throws at me. Then I focus on my gratitude for 15 minutes, writing down all the things I have to feel grateful for that day, which sets me up with a positive mindset. Another thing I learned from my lifestyle coach was the value of journaling, so I now set aside 10 minutes each day to just write down everything that's going on in my life right now, and all my thoughts and feelings about it – good or bad. For me, it's a kind of brain-dump, a way of releasing everything before I face the world.

These tools enable me to start my day feeling refreshed and invigorated – a far cry from the stressed, frantic person I used to be. They may not be what works for everyone; for some, it might be about having a relaxing bath, listening to music or spending time in nature. But whatever it is, building in me-time, doing something to invest in your state of mind and reduce stress, is essential.

And above all, get a sense of balance. Don't put everything into one part of your life, because if things go wrong in that area, you'll wake up one day and realise you've got nothing else.

You are more than a list of your achievements. You are more than your CV. You're worth investing in as a human being. So start making some deposits.

'Love all, trust a few, do wrong to none.' William Shakespeare

7

THE SEARCH FOR TRUE
LOVE AND A HAPPY ENDING

I had worked out what really mattered to me in life. I had sorted out my career. I had learnt to have a sense of balance and not make work everything. I was genuinely starting to experience happiness and joy again, something I would never have thought possible that day I almost drove my car into a wall. I looked at the eight areas of life that I always worked on with my clients, and I realised that they were firing on all cylinders now. Except for one: romance.

It was still my Achilles' heel, the one area of my life that I was beginning to think would never move forward. Towards the end, my marriage had been so unhappy, and the breakup so painful, that the mere thought of getting serious with anyone new made me shudder. I'd started going on a few dates, even sleeping with a few people, but it never went any further than that. The hurt I still felt went so deep that I never let myself get too attached.

One day I started following a personal trainer on Instagram

called Amanda Branco. She had over 40,0000 followers, and it was easy to see why. She was a stunningly beautiful Brazilian girl, with glossy thick hair, big brown eyes and a body to die for. I was amazed when I uploaded a workout video and she clicked 'like'.

Encouraged, I sent her a direct message.

Amanda Branco. I am Tim Cooper. How have we not met yet?

I knew it was cheeky, but something in me was feeling brave that day.

Ha ha ha! she replied. *I don't know how we've not met yet.*

We got chatting and I realised she worked for the same chain of gyms that I had worked for. I told her I'd heard about a workout challenge that was happening at the gym and offered to send her a link to a video about it.

Give me your number and I'll WhatsApp it to you, I wrote.

It was a bit of an obvious ruse to get her phone number, but nevertheless she agreed, and I sent her the video.

Then I didn't message her again. A day went past. My brain was whirling: here was an incredibly attractive woman with whom I felt an immediate connection. Our chat so far had been easy and fun. There was nothing stopping me from messaging her again. Except there was.

There was the feeling that this might be different from the casual dates I'd been on. There was the knowledge, at the back of my mind, that this might go somewhere. And if it did, I would be back on the road to commitment and therefore to getting hurt again, just as I had with Claire.

I had managed to get myself away from so many aspects of my old toxic life. I had rejected the values of that world. I had spent time soul searching and working out what my true values were. I had worked hard with my lifestyle coach to find my true calling in life. I had got rid of all my old friends and found new ones.

But now I had to move on from another, even deeper aspect of that former life: my unhappy marriage. I realised that if I didn't finally and completely put it behind me, I would still be living in the past. I still wouldn't really have escaped from that life. I would still be living in it mentally, even if I wasn't in that house anymore, lying next to my ex-wife at night. And if that was the case, how could anyone new possibly come into my life? It wouldn't be fair to them.

I'd worked so hard to get where I was. I'd faced my demons in every other area. If I had the strength to do that, to come back from the dead, then I could do this. I was ready.

I picked up my phone.

Amanda, I wrote, *I'd like to take you out for a smoothie.*

The girl was a personal trainer, after all.

That would be great! she messaged back.

And from that moment it was so easy. There was no game playing. No bullshit. I would message her, and she would message me back. I didn't keep her waiting, and she didn't play it cool. We started messaging every day, sometimes for hours, sometimes late into the night. I wanted to find out everything about her, and she wanted to know all about me.

After cutting so many toxic people out of my life, I'd become very picky about who I let in. I was so much more aware of whether people I met shared my values, and I could tell early on that this was someone who did. She was a family orientated person: she FaceTimed her mum back in Brazil every day and used the money she earned to fly her little sister and nephew over to England on holidays. She didn't like to talk about shallow stuff; when she asked me questions it was things like, "What's important to you?" not, "How's your day been?" This was someone who was interested in self-growth and in other people. We were having the kind of meaningful conversations about ourselves that I had in my lifestyle coaching. We never once talked about whether we owned property or cars, or how much money we earned.

We agreed to meet at Starbucks in Stratford, near the gym. I got there early and sat waiting with a coffee, and as the minutes went by I was feeling increasingly nervous. What if this online connection didn't translate into the real world? Could this amazingly beautiful woman really want me?

Then out of nowhere I felt a hand on my shoulder, and it was Amanda – looking even more stunning than in her pictures. She said hello, put her arm around me and gave me a hug. It was so warm. It was so Brazilian. It was so un-English. And it was so what I needed. After everything I'd been through, I realised I really needed someone to give me a cuddle.

We wandered down to a little café I knew, where we both ordered poached eggs on toast with avocado for brunch and I bought her that smoothie I had promised her. The conversation flowed, just as it had online, and everything felt so relaxed and natural. *This is it*, I realised. *I've met someone I really, really like. And now I'm screwed.*

I'm screwed because as soon as I tell her I've been divorced she's going to run a mile. Why would a girl like this want someone who comes with all that baggage? Girls want to meet someone who hasn't already walked someone else up the aisle. Who hasn't already done it all with someone else and got it wrong. I looked at this lovely girl sitting opposite me, sipping on her smoothie, and thought that I just couldn't do it.

But one thing all my experiences had taught me was that there was no point in trying to be someone I wasn't. I'd done that in the past, and it had made me miserable. And OK, I'd made a heck of a lot of mistakes in my life. But I also knew I was proud of the way I'd managed to come back from the mess I'd got myself into, that I was proud of how I'd managed to learn from those mistakes. If I was going into this, it had to be with honesty and integrity. I would have to bite the bullet, and risk losing her.

"Look," I said, "there's something I need to tell you."

"I know," she replied. "You're divorced."

"What?" I spluttered.

"My friend knows you from the gym," she explained. "And you know why I'm here? Because she and her friends and everyone who knows you have so many great things to say about you. About your smile, your willingness to help everyone all the time, your energy. My friend said, 'You've *got* to go out with this guy, Amanda. He's a catch.'"

I couldn't believe what I was hearing. She already knew – and she wanted to go out with me anyway. She wanted to know me because of the person I'd become: the person who'd dragged himself away from his old life, gone into that gym and made the decision to be the best version of himself. The person who'd got hooked on helping people after he had needed help himself. The person I was *because* of the difficult things I'd been through.

After brunch, we decided to go for a walk around Stratford. It was a beautiful, sunny day and we strolled arm in arm through Olympic Park, past the aquatic centre towards the stadium. We were chatting non-stop, and I had never felt so connected to a woman in my whole life.

We walked along the canal, and as we went under a bridge, suddenly Amanda pulled me towards her and kissed me. The kiss floored me – the intensity of it, the passion of it, the romance of it. It was like nothing I'd ever experienced before. I felt, overwhelmingly, like I was home. That is how Amanda made me feel.

She was the missing link in everything I had been building for myself. It was as if, after all this time – after all the hard graft I had put in to build myself back up from scratch, all the self-awareness I had gained and all the growth I had achieved – someone was finally saying, "Congratulations, you've done it. Here's your life back."

I told Amanda everything about my past. I spread my whole life out before her and told her to have a good look at it, and to let me know if there was anything she wasn't comfortable with. I told her about the drink and the drugs and the girls. I told her about losing all my money and almost committing suicide. I felt it was important to go into a new relationship giving every part of myself, not hiding who I was and where I'd come from. It was the only way for us to truly connect. And do you know what? She didn't flinch. The pay-off was that I always felt totally relaxed with Amanda. I wasn't trying to be anything other than myself.

I had found someone who shared my true values: family, loyalty, trust, sincerity, self-development and helping others. I'd found someone who had a similar blueprint to me. I didn't have to force myself into a different mould to make our lives together work.

Things moved fast. Amanda and I didn't spend much time apart. I would drive to her flat in London from Hertfordshire to pick her up after she finished work at the gym and she would stay over. Inevitably, soon we started to think it would make much more sense for us to live in the same place. Amanda had a flat in Kensington, in the area that many of my new clients were based, so we talked about me leaving my flat and moving in with her.

Despite my love for Amanda, it wasn't easy for me to make that leap. A part of me still associated commitment with my marriage, and it brought me out in a cold sweat. But I also knew that I was always telling my clients that the thing about past experiences is that they're often out of date. This feeling was from the past, a past that I had already left behind in every other way.

So one day I went home and started sorting through my things. I still had lots of clothes and shoes from my old life: designer labels I no longer wore, smart shoes that I didn't need. Instead of packing them, I started putting them all into bin liners.

My mum came round to see me.

"What are you doing?" she asked, astonished. "You can't get rid of these."

"Mum," I replied, "I haven't worn them for months. I'm going to take them to charity so that someone else can have the benefit of them. They're not who I am now."

It was the final spring clean I needed before my fresh start with Amanda. I arrived at her flat with just a few suitcases. And as soon as I started moving my stuff in, I knew it felt right.

My new life with Amanda is so different to my old one. The flat we live in now is a fraction of the size of the house I once owned. It isn't cool and minimal, it's lived in. We've got two dogs, Bella and Brian, and if they want to jump on the sofa, they can. If they want to get on the bed, they can. I'm not worried about whether they knock something over or leave a mark, because I love the dogs more than the furniture or the carpets.

My old life was about keeping my expensive house looking

perfect. I spent my weekends mowing the lawn to make it look immaculate, or cleaning my sports cars until they gleamed. Now my weekends are all about spending quality time with Amanda. We start the day with a smoothie (of course), and then we take the dogs for a walk in Hyde Park. We love nothing more than watching them rolling in mud and having a laugh at the silly things they get up to. We have a pub lunch at our local, and then we come home and eat the cheapest Neapolitan ice cream from Tesco, just because it's our favourite.

We constantly do romantic things for each other, but it's not about buying her diamonds or designer shoes. It's about things that don't cost any money: running baths, lighting candles, cooking for each other. I don't have any of the material things I had in my marriage, but I'm so much more fulfilled. I no longer have to pretend to be something I'm not.

My real life is finally showing its true colours – and it's a life that I have crafted for myself. A life in which, finally, I am in tune with my authentic self, with my true values, and am living in balance.

That's something you can achieve too, no matter how far off the path you feel you have strayed. You have an authentic self inside of you just waiting to blossom, to show you all that you are capable of. All you have to do is tune in and listen to it – and find the right people to support you on your journey.

If a man who thought his only option was smashing himself into a wall can create the life of his dreams, then – believe me – anyone can.

One weekend, after Amanda and I had been together for a year, I said, "How about we go over to the park and get some videos of us and the dogs?"

"OK," she said.

It was a beautiful summer's day, and we headed over and started strolling towards our favourite spot by a big tree. Amanda went to the loo, and while she was in there I happened to see one of her friends passing by.

"Oh hi mate, could you do me a favour?" I asked. "Amanda's just about to come out of the toilet. Could you hold the camera and film us together?"

"Sure," the guy said.

Amanda re-emerged, and saw me fiddling with something on one of the dogs' collars.

"Brian's got something on him I want you to have a look at," I said.

She bent down and saw that there was a white ribbon tied to his collar. On the ribbon was something small and bright, sparkling in the sun.

I bent down on one knee to untie the ribbon, and off slid a beautiful engagement ring. Amanda clapped her hand to her mouth.

"Amanda," I said, "from the moment I met you I knew you were the one. I knew it. Will you be my wife?"

"Yes," she said quietly.

"We didn't hear that, try it again!" called her friend.

"Yes!" Amanda shouted, laughing.

I slipped the ring onto her finger and drew her close to me.

As I did, it was as if the tide went out. The last of the weight of my old life was unloaded from me, and there was nothing left but lightness and love.

'We keep passing unseen through little moments of other people's lives.' Robert M. Pirsig

'A smile is happiness you'll find right under your nose.' Tom Wilson

DREAM BIG AND ACHIEVE YOUR GOALS

INTRODUCTION

Do you remember how much you used to dream when you were a kid? Can put your hand on your heart and say that you're still dreaming in the same way today? If the answer is no, now's your time to start dreaming again.

'If you think you can or can't, you're right.'
– Henry Ford

Our pasts are made up of thousands of experiences, involving adversity and success and everything in between. These experiences have a considerable influence over whether we feel good enough to achieve what we want from life.

Although our past experiences can guide us through situations in the present, allowing us to identify warning signs and thus helping us to avoid repeating mistakes, they can also result in us missing out on life-changing opportunities.

The thing to remember about past experiences is that they are now out of date. It's time for you to create new ones that will challenge you and help you grow. So how about this: right now, today, let's start to THINK BIG. Let's create some new experiences full of happiness and joy.

Some of the greatest human beings to have ever graced this planet, who changed the shape of the world we live in, started out with a dream. Martin Luther King, Stephen Hawking, Winston Churchill and Mother Theresa all had a dream, a vision that was far bigger than what we term a 'goal'. Of course, there's plenty of time for goals and for engineering your life – and I'm a big believer in measuring your goals, as you will have discovered throughout this book. However, it's also vital to learn how to really dream, and dream big.

It's the dreams of the greats that have made the world what it is today. Now it's your turn.

Effective and Efficient Planning

I'm sure you've heard it before: *It's not the lack of time, it's the lack of priority.*

In a world where we can Amazon Prime our lives, it's quite easy to fall into the trap of thinking, *I'm just too busy.* However, this is usually down to a lack of planning rather than a genuine lack of time. Things rarely get stuck because of a lack of time; they get stuck because you haven't *allocated* time. In order to be successful, you need to have an effective and efficient plan in place. It's the planning itself that creates clarity and allows you to gain perspective; it also allows you to understand where you are right now. Effective and efficient planning is the first step we need to take to reach our dreams.

Emotional Goal Setting

So many people fail when it comes to setting goals. Why is that? They truly desire to make that change in their life, but they hit a wall of resistance when the challenges start to become real.

So what do you need in order to reach your goals? "Motivation!" I hear you say. Not so fast: motivation actually comes last. It's the *hunger* to reach that goal that's first in line. You may be reading this and thinking, *Wait a minute, Tim. I am hungry to reach this goal; I just find it hard to be consistent or disciplined.*

And therein lies the problem: many people lose interest in achieving their goals after a certain amount of time. In my experience, this is because in order to reach your goals you need to have an emotional attachment to them. One of the quickest ways to identify this is to ask yourself, *Is this goal in alignment with my values?*

Our values determine what we stand for. They can represent our uniqueness, our individuality. Values play a huge part in our behaviour, and when we honour our own core values consistently, we experience fulfilment. If our goals aren't in line with our values, it's no wonder we don't achieve them: we simply don't want it badly enough. Deep down, it doesn't mean enough to us. We might think it does at the time, but when the going gets tough and it's time to dig deep, we just give up!

Think about this when setting your next goal.

Visualisation

Trust yourself. You know more than you think you do. Visualisation is about building the picture!

Many years ago, Helen Keller was asked if she thought there was anything worse than being blind. She quickly replied that there was something much worse. She said, "The most pathetic person in the world is a person who has their sight but no vision."

You cannot hit a target that you can't see. Creating a vision of yourself is the first step towards achieving the life you dream of: it's the power of creation. Everything that's ever been created started with an idea. Figure out what you want. Visualise it.

An important aspect of visualisation is ensuring that all the different components of your life – health and fitness, family and relationships, fun and job, romance, physical environment, money and finances, career and work and personal development – support your overall vision. Only when you look into your own heart will your vision align with your values and principles.

Remember: your imagination is a preview of your life's coming attractions. We all have free will, so if you're not happy with a certain aspect of your life, change them. Ask yourself, *What would I do if I knew I couldn't fail?* Get really specific: what is your passion? What do you see your future self looking like?

As in every area of our lives there are some fundamentals that need to be in place to pave the road for tomorrow, the next year and the next decade. Creating a vision and asking yourself specific question about your future is one of those fundamentals.

Remember: do not settle for the life you are living unless you are completely satisfied with it.

Mindfulness

'What lies behind us and what lies before us are small matters compared to what lies within us.'
– Ralph Waldo Emerson

I'm a huge fan of being clear about your destination, setting up daily intentions and taking the relevant courses of action to help you achieve your dreams. Having said that, it's just as important to understand your foundations, what's moulded you into the person you are today and why you currently behave the way you do.

The only thing that's completely real about your journey is the steps you are taking at this exact moment, because this moment – right now – is all there ever is.

Practicing mindfulness allows us to stop, breathe and concentrate on the present moment. It allows us to move away from the anxious thoughts about our predicted future or unpleasant past. When you practice mindfulness, you start to move out of your own head and learn to notice the beauty that surrounds you in this world, the small pleasures that can too often pass you by. In a world full of distractions and pressures, it's easy to become a slave to your thoughts, which sit outside of the here and now. Practicing mindfulness gently teaches you to become aware of each and every moment as it happens – which, in time, allows you to become connected to the truest, wisest parts of yourself.

Accepting each moment as it happens is the key to learning to accept yourself as you are. It is the key to accepting others for who *they* are rather than judging them, and to being kind to yourself instead of wishing things were different all the time. It is the perfect formula for a calm, healthy mind.

Mindfulness

The Wheel of Life

Many of us can feel overwhelmed when it comes to starting out on a new journey. It can seem like we have a huge mountain to climb. Determining where to start can be just as daunting as the journey itself; no wonder why so many of us fail to even get started.

The Wheel of Life is the perfect tool for reflecting on how far you have come and what you have learned on your journey so far. It's about being completely honest about where you are in your life right now, and about the size of the gap between where you are and where you want to be. It not only allows you to determine where you want to go, but it creates balance, happiness and success.

When using the Wheel of Life, the idea is to score or rank your rate of satisfaction in each of the eight main areas of your life (for more information on these, see the following section). Doing this allows you to reflect and gain a sense of balance.

In the following section, you will find an activity titled The Life Board. This is an extension of the Wheel of Life that allows you to delve deeper into why your wheel looks the way it does. The Wheel highlights how successful you feel each area of your life is at the present time; the Life Board takes that information and allows you to drill down into how you can improve each of those areas.

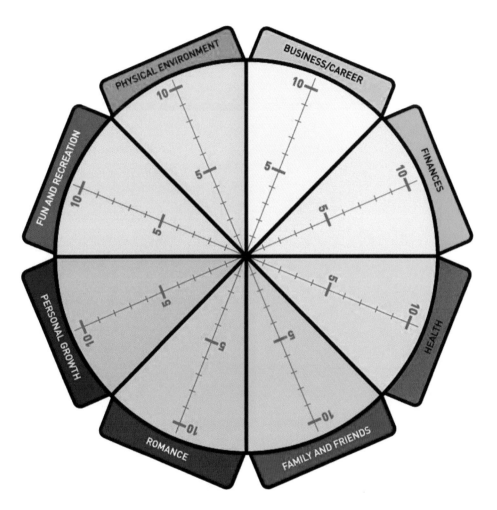

The Life Wheel

Fulfilment

ACTIVITY:
THE LIFE BOARD

Setting Up Your Life Board

• You will need a large piece of card or paper, preferably A1 size, and a set of multi-coloured Sharpie pens or colouring pens. You can purchase these from an art or stationary shop.

• Lay the board out on the floor or on a flat surface.

• Choose your favourite colour pen and write in the middle of the board, in large capital letters, 'MY LIFE'. Now circle it!

• Now it's time to start equally dividing the board into eight, to represent the eight main areas of life. Start by writing 'Personal Development and Growth' at the top left-hand side of the board, and keep going until you have all eight areas represented. See the diagram for an example.

You are now ready to start dreaming! What do you feel is currently missing from each area of your life? How do you see your future self? Your best self? Visualise what you want to change in each of these eight areas and write it down.

Let me help you out with some examples:

Personal Development and Growth

- I want to take more action in my life and stop procrastinating.
- I'd like to build more confidence.
- I want to have more self-belief and be less controlled by fear of failure.

Money and Finance

- I want to have financial freedom.
- I want to give others the opportunity to experience financial freedom.

Family and Relationships

- I'd like to spend more time with my spouse.
- I want to make more time for my parents as they get older.

Remember that within each category you are trying to visualise the best possible version of your future self – the person you want to become.

Most people I've worked with on the Life Board have ended up with around 10 things they would like to improve in each of the eight areas – though however many you come up with is fine. This exercise is totally specific to you. It's your board, so you do you!

HEALTH/FITNESS

WORK/CAREER

MONEY/FINANCE

FAMILY/RELATIONSHIPS

MY LIFE

PHYSICAL ENVIRONMENT

PERSONAL DEVELOPMENT/PERSONAL
GROWTH

FUN/JOY

ROMANCE

The Life Board: an example

Setting Your Goals

The next part of this exercise is slightly more challenging.

1.   Look at each of the components in your life that you would like to change or improve upon and pick out your top five. Scaling the list down in this way will help you identify what's most important to you: what really needs optimum focus and requires immediate action.

Note: you may find that you have areas that cross over. For example, self-belief, self-esteem and confidence could all potentially fit under the same banner. If this is the case for you, then you can start to think about grouping areas together.

OK. By now your board should be looking ready for some goals to be put in place.

2.   For each category, we're going to create five courses of action – we can also call them 'intentions' – that will help you improve on or change each of the areas you've identified. For example, in Personal Development and Growth, write down a course of action that will enable you to achieve higher self-esteem and remove that niggling fear of failure. You'll need to really dig deep and be honest with yourself. What's been holding you back from achieving this up until now? Think back to a time when you experienced success in this area of your life. What were you doing differently? What habits did

you have in place? What were your daily intentions?

If you simply cannot remember, or you've never experienced success in this area of your life, try to envision the reverse of how you are currently living. For example, if, under Personal Development and Growth, you have written something like, *I'd like to feel more confident in my clothes*, but you can't remember ever having felt confident in your clothes before, write down as an action point along the lines of, *I want to work out four or five times a week because I know that if I get into shape, I will feel more confident in my clothes and will feel happier in myself.*

Each of your five goals will need a timeframe and a resource that will help you achieve them. You may feel that you don't have many resources; however, in my experience the problem is a lack of resourcefulness rather than a lack of resources. This is another time for you to really dig deep and tap into everything and everyone you know to help you achieve your goal.

What Your Goals Will Look Like

By the time you are finished with your Life Board, each area should have five goals laid out and look something like this:

Personal Development and Growth

Goal: I want to feel more confident in my clothes.

Action/Intention: I will commit to working out with a friend or personal trainer five mornings a week.

Timescale: I will achieve this by 8am every day.

For each of your eight areas, you should have identified:

1. The goal (in this case, the goal is to feel more confident in your clothes)

2. The action you intend to take to achieve the goal (in this case, there is a commitment to work out five days a week)

3. The timescale in which you intend to act to achieve the goal (in this case, the workout must be completed by 8am every day)

4. The resources you will tap into to help you achieve the goal (in this instance, the resource is a friend or personal trainer).

HEALTH/FITNESS

FAMILY/RELATIONSHIPS

PERSONAL DEVELOPMENT/PERSONAL GROWTH

1. I want to take more action
2. Build my confidence
3. Believe in myself
4. More focused
5. Disciplined
6. More present
7. Be decisive
8. Over come fear of failure

WORK/CAREER

MONEY/FINANCE

MY LIFE

PHYSICAL ENVIRONMENT

FUN/JOY

ROMANCE

An example of the Life Board with all vision

PERSONAL DEVELOPMENT/PERSONAL
GROWTH

1. Take more action
2. Remove fear of failure
3. Be disciplined
4. Focused
5. Decisive

FAMILY/RELATIONSHIPS

HEALTH/FITNESS

FUN/JOY

MY LIFE

WORK/CAREER

ROMANCE

PHYSICAL ENVIRONMENT

MONEY/FINANCE

An example of the Life Board with five goals

'The aim of education is the knowledge not of facts, but of values.' William S. Burroughs

THE 30-DAY
JOURNAL CHALLENGE

'You cannot escape the responsibility of tomorrow by evading it today.' Abraham Lincoln

DAY 1

Today I will let go of:

1. ....
2. ....
3. ....

What person will I commit to become over the next 30 days?

....
....
....

What positive effect will this have on others around me?

....
....
....

'Happiness cannot be traveled to, owned, earned, worn or consumed. Happiness is the spiritual experience of living every minute with love, grace and gratitude.' Denis Waitley

DAY 2

What is getting in the way of living the life I want?

1. ....
2. ....
3. ....

Why is it important to overcome these obstacles?

....
....
....

How will/can I improve my focus in this area?

....
....
....

'Some people dream of success, while other people get up every morning and make it happen.'
Wayne Huizenga

DAY 3

What opportunities would improving my financial situation bring?

1. ....
2. ....
3. ....

What resources could I put in place to help me achieve this?

....
....
....

Why is this important to me?

....
....
....

'Physical fitness is not only one of the most important keys to a healthy body, it is the basis of dynamic and creative intellectual activity.' John F. Kennedy

DAY 4

What are my fitness goals for the next 30 days?

1. ....
2. ....
3. ....

Who will I share these goals with? Who will I tell about them?

....
....
....

How will it feel when I achieve these goals?

....
....
....

'Nothing you wear is more important than your smile.' Connie Stevens

DAY 5

Write about a time when somebody did something nice for you. How did it feel?

....

....

....

What am I grateful for today?

1. ....

2. ....

3. ....

How can I be more present in my relationships?

1. ....

2. ....

3. ....

'Nature's beauty is a gift that cultivates appreciation and gratitude.' Louie Schwartzberg

DAY 6

What is the most fun I have ever had?

....

....

....

What three things would I do if I wasn't afraid?

1. ....

2. ....

3. ....

If I could change one thing about my present life, what would it be?

....

....

....

'The good thing about the start is that you're never there again.' Tim Cooper

DAY 7

What is my wildest dream?

....
....
....

How would I like to make this world a better place?

....
....
....

What will I commit to giving back to the world over the next
30 days?

....
....
....

'Success is not final, failure is not fatal: it is the courage to continue that counts.'
Winston Churchill

DAY 8

What is the single most difficult lesson that I have had to learn over the past year?

....
....
....

Why did it have so much impact on my life?

....
....
....

How will I make sure it never happens again?

....
....
....

'You gain strength, courage and confidence by every experience in which you really stop to look fear in the face. You are able to say to yourself, "I lived through this horror. I can take the next thing that comes along."' *Eleanor Roosevelt*

DAY 9
WORK AND CAREER

What is my main career goal for the next six months?

....

....

....

How will achieving this make me feel?

....

....

....

What are the long-term benefits of achieving this goal?

....

....

....

'Time is of more value than money. You can get more money, but you cannot get more time.'
Jim Rohn

DAY 10
MONEY AND FINANCE

What is my relationship with money like?

....

....

Improving this area will allow me to:

1. ....

2. ....

3. ....

What tools can I use to ensure I stay on track?

....

....

What three things would help me achieve happiness in this area?

....

....

'Every day is a journey, and the journey itself is home.' Matsuo Basho

DAY 11
PERSONAL DEVELOPMENT AND GROWTH

What three words best describe my mindset right now?

....

....

How can I connect more deeply with myself?

....

....

What areas of my life do I need to take more action in?

....

....

What positive effects will taking this action have on others around me?

....

....

What can I do to ensure that I start this today?

....

....

'A smile is happiness you'll find right under your nose.' Tom Wilson

DAY 12
FUN AND JOY

When was the last time I cried with laughter?

....

....

....

Why was it so funny?

....

....

....

Who did I last smile at?

....

....

....

What could I do to have more fun today?

....

....

....

'Holidays are about experiences and people, and tuning into what you feel like doing at that moment. Enjoy not having to look at a watch.' Evelyn Glennie

DAY 13
PHYSICAL ENVIRONMENT

If I visualise my perfect day, what does it look like?

....

....

How could changing my environment benefit my performance at work?

....

....

When was the last time I took a holiday?

....

....

Where is my dream travel destination?

....

....

What steps are in place to ensure that I visit there?

1. ....

2. ....

3. ....

'You will only find your true values when you look deep within your heart.' Tim Cooper

DAY 14
FAMILY AND RELATIONSHIPS

What could I do to make my closest relationships more satisfying?

1. ....
2. ....
3. ....

How would achieving this make me feel?

....

....

What could I put in place so that I remember to do this every day?

....

....

When was the last time I said "I love you"?

....

If I was to connect more deeply in my relationships, what effect would this have on others around me?

....

....

'Take care of your body. It's the only place you have to live.' *Jim Rohn*

DAY 15
HEALTH AND FITNESS

What lesson can I learn today to make me a better person tomorrow?

....

....

If my body could talk what would it be saying right now?

....

....

Today I finally let go of...

....

What do I say to myself about myself?

1. ....

2. ....

3. ....

What is my current workout routine?

....

....

'What we want is far less important that how we want to feel.' Tim Cooper

DAY 16

What does it mean to be focused?

....

....

How do I choose to work on my actions?

....

....

What moved me ahead in the past?

   1. ....

   2. ....

   3. ....

When am I dishonest with myself?

   1. ....

   2. ....

   3. ....

'Affirmation without discipline is the beginning of delusion.' Jim Rohn

DAY 17

What obstacles to change have I run into over the past week?

....

....

....

Do I need to change my situation or change the way I respond to it?

....

....

When was my last big win?

....

....

....

How do I celebrate my wins?

1. ....

2. ....

3. ....

'Gravitation is not responsible for people falling in love.' Albert Einsten

DAY 18

Describe your social life. How satisfied are you with it?

....

....

....

Paint a picture of what a great family life will look like to you.

....

....

....

Where do I need to take better care of my mind, emotions or body?

....

....

....

What skills can I commit to developing over the next 30 days?

....

....

....

'Honesty is the first chapter in the book of wisdom.' Thomas Jefferson

DAY 19

What could I do differently to be better aligned with my values?

....

....

....

What could I do to elevate my energy today?

....

....

....

What is my very next step?

....

....

....

How will this have a positive impact on others?

....

....

....

'Your determination, selflessness and courage have brought the freedom struggle towards its fulfilment.' Gerry Adams

DAY 20

What change in my thinking needs to take place in order for me to become the person I desire to be?

....

....

....

What does success mean to me?

1. ....

2. ....

3. ....

What actions am I avoiding?

....

....

....

How committed am I to achieving success? (Give a percentage.)

....

....

'Either write something worth reading or do something worth writing about.'
Benjamin Franklin

DAY 21

Today I will focus on:

....

....

When was the last time I finished a book?

....

....

....

Today I am grateful for:

....

....

List five positive affirmations:

1. ....

2. ....

3. ....

4. ....

5. ....

'How people treat you is their karma; how you react is yours.' Wayne Dyer

DAY 22

What are my intentions for this week?

....

....

....

Is there anything in work or life that I'm denying?

....

....

....

What do I most want to get out of this week?

....

....

....

Are there adjustments that I can make to my attitude?

....

....

....

'Life is far too important a thing ever to talk seriously about.' Oscar Wilde

DAY 23

Today I will start:

....

....

....

What will I do to improve my fitness for the rest of this week?

....

....

....

When was the last time I set a personal record?

....

....

....

How happy am I with my nutrition?

....

....

....

'Success is where preparation and opportunity meet.' Bobby Unser

DAY 24

My five mini goals for today are:

1. ....
2. ....
3. ....
4. ....
5. ....

Achieving these will make me feel:

....

....

....

Who can I tell about these goals to make me accountable?

....

....

....

'Health is the greatest gift, contentment the greatest wealth, faithfulness the best relationship.'
Buddha

DAY 25

What is my ultimate financial goal for the next 30 days?

....

....

Who can help me achieve this?

....

....

....

Why is this important to me?

1. ....

2. ....

3. ....

Describe what being organised looks like to you.

1. ....

2. ....

3. ....

'If people like you, they'll listen to you, but if they trust you, they'll do business with you.'
Zig Ziglar

DAY 26

On a scale of one to 10, how satisfied am I with my career?

....

....

....

Is my current career path supporting who I am and who I want to be?

....

....

What is motivating me to achieve success in this area?

1. ....

2. ....

3. ....

How do I handle rejection in the workplace?

....

....

....

'Your diet is a bank account. Good food choices are good investments.' Bethenny Frankel

DAY 27

What's the one thing I've been putting off?

....

....

How would I feel if I finally got around to doing it?

....

....

How would achieving this have a positive impact on my relationships?

....

....

What needs to be in place to start with?

1. ....

2. ....

3. ....

What resources could I use to help me achieve this?

....

....

'Where there is no vision, there is no hope.' George Washington Carver

DAY 28

What will I remove from my life that's no longer serving me?

....

....

....

What effect will that have on me?

....

....

....

Why?

....

....

....

What emotions have I overcome this week?

....

....

....

'Optimism is the faith that leads to achievement. Nothing can be done without hope and confidence.' Helen Keller

DAY 29

What would it mean to me to live life on my terms?

....

....

....

What needs to be in place to achieve this?

   1. ....

   2. ....

   3. ....

What will I do to celebrate this?

....

....

....

What is my favourite quote?

....

....

....

'A successful life is not built on your ability to add but on your ability to remove.'
Tim Cooper

DAY 30

How successful have the last 30 days been? (Give a percentage.)

....

....

What will I do to ensure that the next 30 days are even better?

....

....

....

Who will make me accountable for this?

....

....

....

Why is it important to keep up this momentum?

....

....

....

Over the next 90 days I will commit to:

....

....

....

StoryTerrace®

Printed in Great Britain
by Amazon